Volcano Project

written by Michael Steer
photographed by Russell Millard

Contents

Introduction		3
What Is a Volcano?		4
A Volcano Project		8
Research Ideas		23
Index/Glossary		24

Introduction

Why does a volcano erupt? How powerful is a volcanic eruption? What makes a volcano active, dormant, or extinct?

In this book you will learn the answers to these questions. You will also learn how to create your own active volcano.

What Is a Volcano?

Deep inside the earth, rock becomes so hot that it melts. This molten rock is called **magma**.

When magma bursts through the earth's crust, it causes an **eruption**. During an eruption, magma spurts out and flows above ground.

Fact File 1

On May 20, 1883, a volcano called Krakatoa exploded in Indonesia. It was heard over 2,485 miles away.

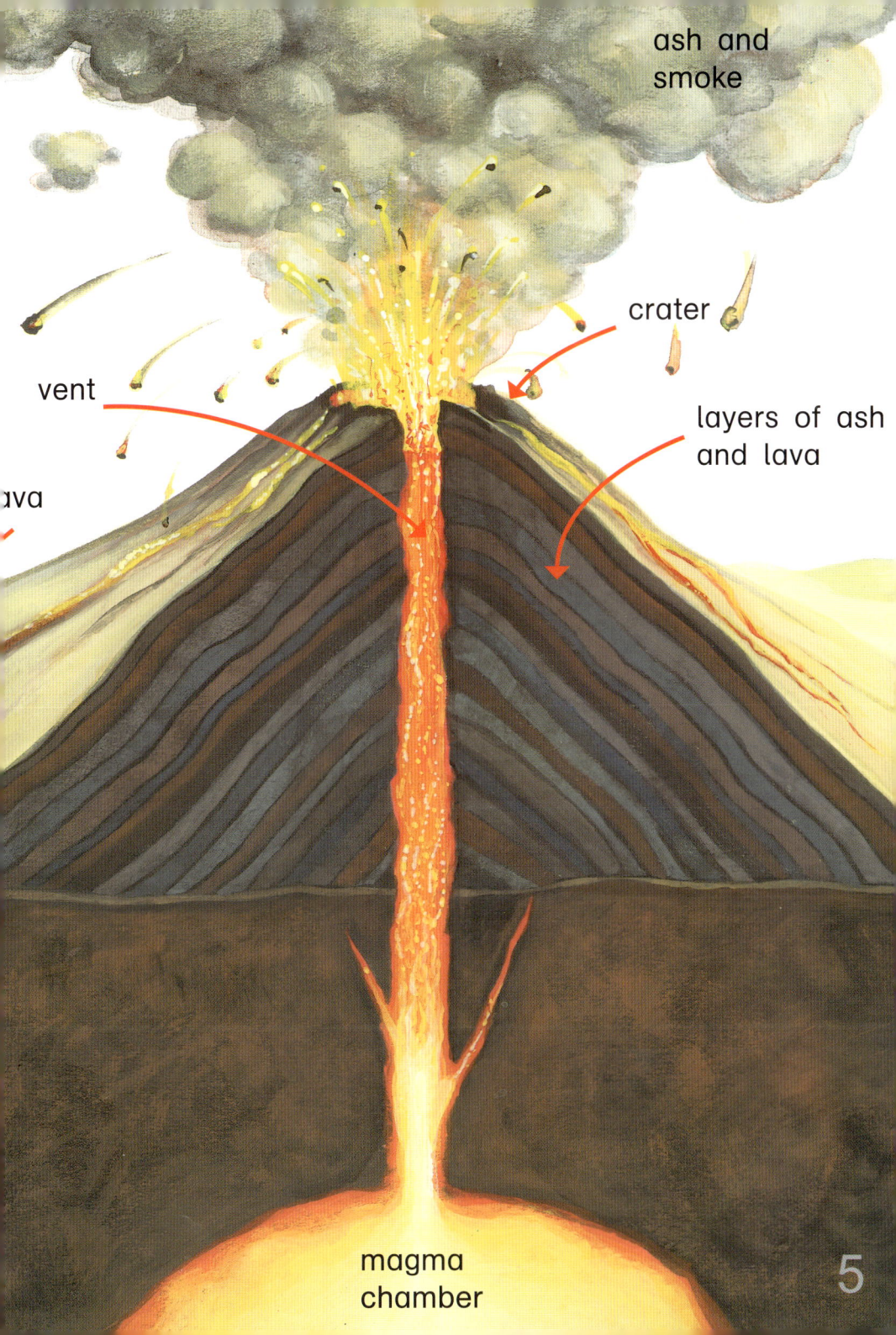

Once the magma reaches the surface of the earth, it is called **lava**. Lava is so hot that it is bright red. Each time there is an eruption, new lava flows over layers of older lava that has cooled and turned to rock. Gradually, these different layers of lava build up and grow into a volcano.

Fact File 2

Mt. Etna is a volcano in Sicily. It has been erupting for a half million years.

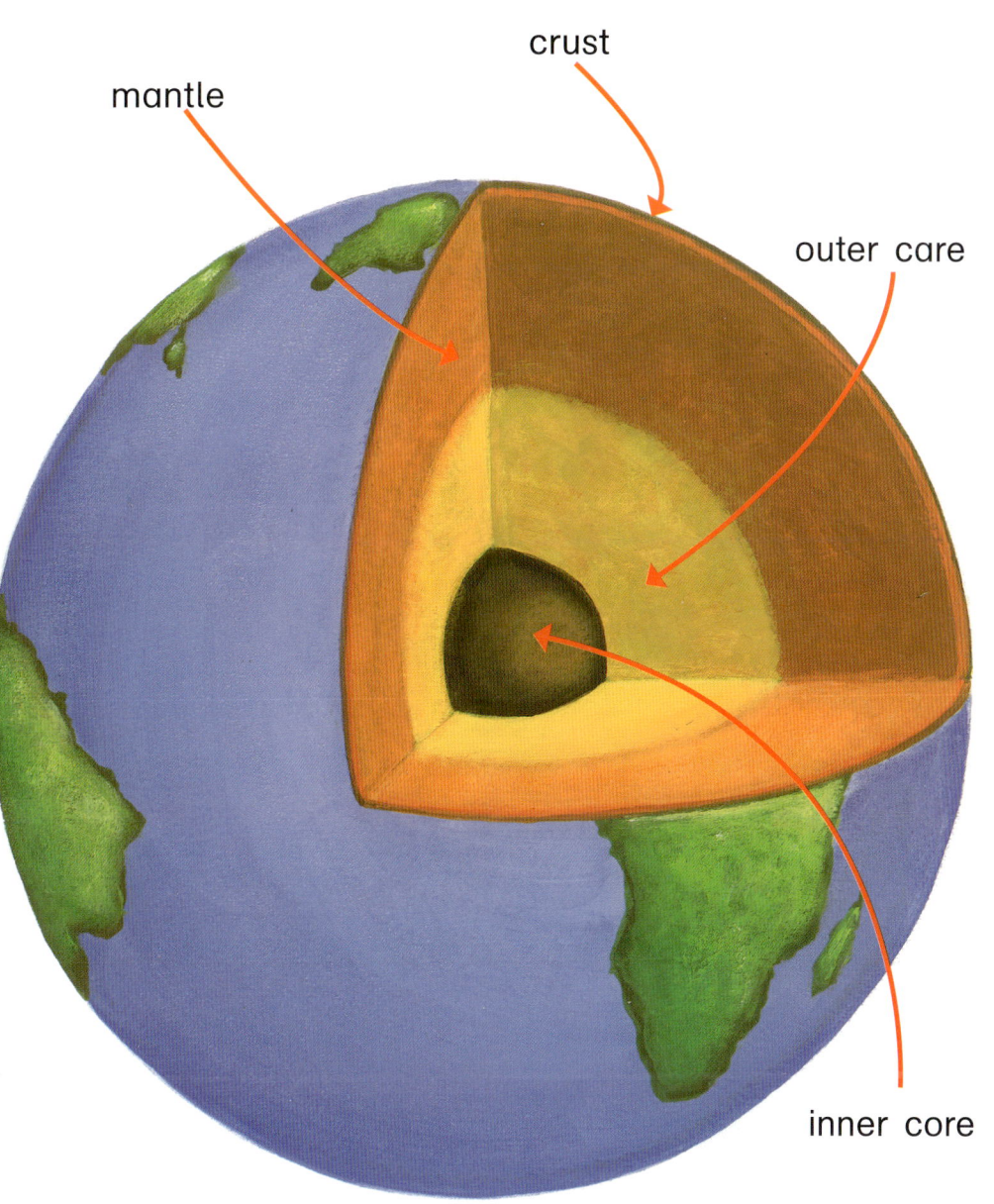

A Volcano Project

You can make a model volcano.

What You Need

    liquid dishwashing detergent
    baking soda
    vinegar
    red food coloring
    water
    a plastic cup between 4 inches and 6 inches high
    a bucket of sand
    play dough or plaster
    a measuring cup
    a board or plate
    white, black, and red paint

Fact File 3

A volcano called Mt. Vesuvius erupted in Italy in 79 A.D. For about eight hours, huge smoke clouds dumped ash, dust, cinders, and rocks on the town of Pompeii. Many people died as a result.

Building a volcano can be messy. Ask an adult for help.

Instructions

1. Put 1/4 cup of baking soda into the cup. Make sure you measure the right amount.

2. Add 1 ounce of dishwashing liquid and 5 drops of red food coloring to the baking soda.

11

3. Put sand around the cup in the same way that you would build a sandcastle. Make it into a cone shape like a volcano.

13

4. Put a small amount of water around the sides of the volcano so it makes the sand stick together.

5. Add water to your plaster and stir it until the mixture is smooth. The plaster should be wet enough to pour easily and thick enough to stick to the sides of your model volcano.

6. Pour a small amount of plaster down the sides of the volcano until the plaster is 1/2 inch thick. Then let it dry.

7. When the plaster has formed a hard surface around the top of the volcano, paint it with the water-based paint.

Make sure that you let the paint dry.

8. Place small stones and plants at the base of the volcano. If you have small plastic toys, you could put houses and people at the base of the volcano, too.

Fact File 4

If a volcano erupts with lava or gas, or if it makes the ground shake, then we say it is **active**.

If a volcano has not erupted for a long time but could erupt again one day, then we say it is **dormant**. This means it is "sleeping."

If a volcano will never erupt again, then we say it is **extinct**.

9. Call your friends or a parent to share in your experiment!

Pour the vinegar into the top of the bottle and watch as the model volcano comes to life. (When you mix vinegar with baking soda, it makes a lot of foam.)

The red foam will flow down the sides of the model volcano just like the lava from a real volcano.

If you have a video camera, you could make a movie of the eruption to take to school or to show your friends.

Fact File 5

A scientist who studies volcanoes is called a **volcanologist**. This word comes from **Vulcan**, who in Roman mythology was the god of fire and volcanos. Volcanologists can use video cameras, still cameras, and infrared cameras operated by remote control. This is how they can safely watch dangerous things as they happen.